Fighting For Children's Rights

The Story of Lewis Hine

Written by Nancy O'Connor

Flying Start
to Literacy®

Contents

Introduction

The mill foreman crossed his strong arms over his chest and glared at the little man with the camera. "What do you think you're doing here?" he growled. "I have orders not to let troublemakers onto this property."

The photographer was used to this kind of "welcome" when he tried to get into places where children were working.

"I assure you, I'm no troublemaker," said the photographer, but he knew that his photographs would stir up trouble. He was working undercover investigating businesses that used children to do hard and dangerous work for only a few cents a day.

And because he didn't look like a troublemaker, he persuaded the foreman to let him enter the mill.

Workers and the foreman outside a factory in Macon, Georgia, USA. The smallest child in the photograph said he earned 52 cents a day.

Young workers and their boss inside a cotton mill in South Carolina, USA

Girls and boys in the spinning room of a cotton mill
in Fall River, Massachusetts, USA, 1912

Inside, he found a huge room of girls and boys working on industrial machinery. The air was thick with dust and lint. The windows were so filthy, the afternoon sun barely shone through them. Children coughed and wheezed as they worked.

Dirty and dangerous working conditions were common throughout the United States in the early 20th Century. It was not illegal to employ children under 12 to work on farms and in factories, but there were rules about how long children could work and what type of work they could do. Employers, parents and even the children themselves pretended they were older than 12 to get the job. Many were much younger than 12 – some were as young as four or five years old.

The photographer set up his camera. Then he persuaded the foreman to allow one of the girls to be in the picture.

"How old are you?" he quietly asked the girl.

She darted a quick glance at the foreman before she answered. "I'm 12," she said, standing as tall as possible. He knew from looking at her that she was no 12-year-old. More likely, she was only eight or nine. He didn't say anything, but he knew his photo would speak for itself. And it was going to stir up trouble.

Addie Card, a 10-year-old textile worker at a cotton mill in Vermont, USA

Chapter 1

Becoming a photographer

Lewis Hine

Lewis Hine was born on 26 September, 1874, in Wisconsin in the United States. He grew up going to school, doing odd jobs and playing with friends. His father died when he graduated from high school and Hine became the "man of the house". He had to find work to support his mother and sister.

Before he became a photographer, he did a variety of jobs. He worked for a furniture company, but the hours were long, the furniture was heavy and he didn't earn much money. Later, he worked in a bank and then he decided to become a teacher. In 1901, Hine went to teach at a school in New York City.

An apartment building in New York City that Lewis Hine visited to photograph working ▶ families. Sometimes up to eight families lived and worked together in one apartment.

At the school, he started a camera club for the students. He became the school's photographer. After school, Hine took the students from the camera club to the countryside to photograph nature. He also took them around the poorest parts of the city to take pictures of the people who lived there. They witnessed the hardship, poverty and terrible living conditions of families in the slums of New York City. Later in his life, the children of these families would become Hine's photo subjects.

While living in New York City, Hine made many visits to Ellis Island. Ellis Island was where immigrants from around the world arrived by ship to settle in the United States. Hine visited there many times to take photographs of the immigrant families. He set up his camera equipment in the crowded immigration halls and chose a few people at a time to photograph. Hine's Ellis Island pictures showed the anxiety, fear and pride of the many families arriving in the United States, hoping to make new lives for themselves.

A German immigrant family at the registry office at Ellis Island

A group of Italian immigrants in the arrival hall at Ellis Island

As Hine's photography skills increased, so did his reputation. Soon, his photographs were being published in journals and magazines. They began to be seen by many people around the country.

Chapter 2

Working for change

At the beginning of the 20th century, it was common to employ children to do the work of adults. This was called child labour and the law didn't prevent it from happening.

Two girls employed in a cotton mill

Children worked in factories, on farms and in mines. Many worked in dirty, unsafe places. Bosses employed them and paid them much less than they paid adults.

Community groups and unions wanted to abolish child labour. One group was the National Child Labor Committee (NCLC). It employed Lewis Hine as a photographer to take pictures of where and how children were working. The NCLC knew that many children across the United States were being exploited, working for very little money and not going to school. It wanted to investigate children's working conditions and protect their rights.

The NCLC wanted the government to make it illegal to employ children under the age of 14. If the work was dangerous, the law would require workers to be at least 16. The NCLC also wanted to limit the workday to eight hours and to make it compulsory for all children to go to school.

Getting such laws passed and obeyed was difficult. Child labourers were too young to talk back and stand up to their bosses. Young workers were considered cheap labour who didn't often complain.

Lawrence Faircloth and Albert Bartlett (barefoot) worked in a mill for two years, earning 25 cents a day.

Eight-year-old Michael McNelis, a newsie who had just recovered from his second attack of pneumonia, selling papers in a big rainstorm

Lewis Hine and his camera were going to change that. From 1908 to 1918, he travelled around the country photographing and talking to working children. He took photographs of children working on farms, in factories, down mines, at home and on city streets right across the United States. His easy-going nature helped children trust him. Many opened up to him about their lives. Every time he took a photo, he wrote down the children's names, their ages and their stories in a small notebook he kept hidden in his pocket.

In cities like New York, thousands of people lived in poverty. Small apartments were home to two or more families. There was no running water, no toilets and no fire escapes. Entire families, including the children, worked 12 hours a day doing things like sewing, making paper flowers for ladies' hats or crocheting fabric. The few cents they earnt barely bought enough food.

An Italian family crocheting bags while the father is sick in bed.

Chapter 3

The children and their stories

Lewis Hine travelled more than 19,000 kilometres around the United States visiting places children worked. He dressed in a suit and tie and carried a simple box camera and small notebook. He made notes about each photograph he took and decided never to retouch the photos or create fake images.

Five-year-old Helen and her stepsisters hulling strawberries. Helen started work at 6 a.m. and was still hulling strawberries at 6 p.m. the day this photograph was taken.

Eight-year-old Daisy Langford placed caps on cans at Ross' canneries at a rate of 40 per minute, but she found it hard to keep up.

Sometimes Hine was allowed inside a cannery or mill to take pictures. More often, he was forbidden. When that happened, he waited patiently outside the gates and took pictures as young workers arrived in the morning or as they left at the end of the workday. Sometimes children were afraid to talk to Hine. They worried that by allowing him to take their photo, they might lose their jobs. But often the children were proud of the work they did. They felt they were helping their families.

Visiting the workplace

Oyster shuckers and shrimp peelers

Rosie, a seven-year-old oyster shucker who worked all day and had already been shucking oysters for two years

In the American state of Louisiana, Hine met four-year-old Mary, who worked by her mother's side shucking two pots of oysters a day. The dirty, rough oyster shells cut her hands and made them bleed.

In South Carolina, Hine photographed young shrimp peelers. Some young workers started work as early as 5 a.m. and worked for four hours before going to school. Their hands were sore, swollen and sometimes bleeding from the acid in the shrimp shells. At night the workers soaked their swollen and bloody fingers in water and alum (a chemical compound) to toughen them up. The acid from the shrimp shells was so strong that it ate through their leather shoes and their metal buckets.

Six-year-old Josie; six-year-old Bertha; ten-year-old Sophia – oyster shuckers ▶

19

Cotton pickers

Sometimes whole families worked in the cotton fields, dragging around their large sacks of cotton. Many families lived in temporary accommodation because they moved from place to place to find work. One four-year-old cotton picker proudly told Hine she could pick almost four kilograms of cotton a day. Her five-year-old sister could pick 13 kilograms.

Millie, a four-year-old cotton picker

Cleo Campbell, a young cotton picker

Hine discovered that most of the children he met in the cotton fields had so little schooling they didn't know how to write their own names. Some didn't know how old they were. One girl, called Cleo Campbell, told Hine: "I'd rather go to school and then I wouldn't have to work." Cotton pickers worked in the hotter months. It was repetitive and hard work. Workers were on their feet all day, bending over to pick the cotton by hand, dropping it into a bag, then moving on to the next plant.

Breaker boys

Hine photographed breaker boys working in coal mines. These boys worked even though their hands were raw and bloody. Their job was to dig through the coal chutes to pick out the pieces of rock that were mixed in with the good coal. Sometimes the boss prodded or kicked them to make them work faster.

Some boys had to stay underground for ten hours a day. The boys who worked to control the ventilation in the mine spent the whole day in the dark, opening and closing a door. The air in the mines was thick with dust and Hine met many children who had eye problems and lung ailments.

He learnt of the death of a boy named Patrick Kearny in a coal mining accident. During the inquest into Patrick's death, the mine foreman told the court the boy had been 14, but the boy's father admitted his son was actually only nine-and-a-half.

Breaker boys, Pittston, Pennsylvania, USA, January 1911

Street kids

In Hine's own city of New York, there were thousands of orphaned children. These children never went to school and survived by doing odd jobs such as selling chewing gum, peanuts or pencils on the street.

Shoeshiners

Some worked as shoeshine boys carrying wooden boxes filled with shoe polish, brushes and rags to shine people's shoes. They worked six to eight hours a day, and earnt about one dollar a day. Some boys worked until 11.00 o'clock at night.

A shoeshine boy at work

Newsies on the streets of New York City

Newsies

Some children, known as "newsies", sold newspapers. They bought stacks of newspapers every morning and stood on street corners shouting, "Extra! Extra! Read all about it!" Many of these children lived in dormitories where they paid a few cents a night for a bed to sleep in and a meal of soup and bread.

Chapter 4
An enduring legacy

The National Child Labor Committee (NCLC) had begun to publish Lewis Hine's photographs of child workers in magazines and other publications. The pictures showed how companies all around the United States were taking advantage of children by using them as cheap labour.

Hine also set up his own photo exhibits and published pamphlets with photographs and information about child workers. He had hoped to shock and anger people, and he succeeded. People around the country started to realise the laws needed to change.

A National Child Labor Committee pamphlet ▶

CHILD LABOR TO-DAY

WHAT <u>SOCIETY</u> SHOULD DO ABOUT IT

Make Minimum Age 14 Years
Have Higher Age Limit for Dangerous Work
Secure Eight-Hour Workday
Eliminate Night Work
Regulate Street Occupations
Prohibit Homework
Demand Physical and Educational Tests

WHAT <u>YOU</u> CAN DO ABOUT IT

Write your Congressman and Senator
endorsing the Palmer Federal Child Labor
Bill now pending
Join the National Child Labor Committee

Declaration of Dependence

In 1913, the NCLC wrote a document called "The Declaration of Dependence", which was used to protect the rights of children. This document helped ban most forms of child labour and promoted compulsory education for all children. Through his work with the NCLC, Lewis Hine had helped to change the nation's laws.

Lewis Hine said many factories were full of youngsters like this tiny girl who worked as a spinner in a cotton mill in South Carolina, USA

Child labour laws

It took many more years for child labour to be completely abolished in the United States. To the present day, the NCLC continues its work to maintain children's labour rights. In other parts of the world however, there are still many children labouring for long hours and low pay in rug factories, fields, canneries and warehouses. Work still needs to be done to protect them and give them the chance to have an education and a happy childhood.

Lewis Hine felt all children deserved a happy childhood and the opportunity to go to school. Using his camera, he had let the world know how children were suffering. His work made a difference.

Boys of about ten or 11 years of age, on their break from working day shift at a glass factory in Alexandria, Virginia, USA in 1923. Some weeks they worked the night shift.

Conclusion

Although Lewis Hine did not behave like a troublemaker when he argued or talked his way into the worksites of many young Americans, his pictures stirred up enough trouble to help improve the childhoods of future generations of American children.

This mild-mannered man made a difference in the lives of the children he photographed and in the minds of the American public. A collection of over 5000 photographs he took of child workers is now in the Library of Congress in Washington, DC, in the United States. The pictures are a sad reminder of what happened in the early 1900s.

The NCLC continues its fight against child labour today. Every year, the NCLC presents ten individuals with a Lewis Hine Award and $1000 US dollars for their services to young people. These individuals are helping protect the rights of children across the country.

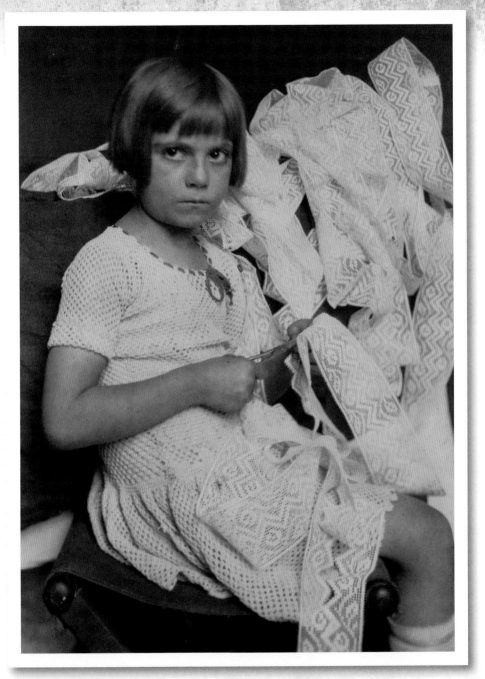

Many families worked long hours at home doing embroidery, beading and sewing.
This girl is cutting lace.

A note from the author

When I was asked to write this book, I didn't know who Lewis Hine was. I had seen a few old black and white photos of children at work in coal mines and of newsies selling their papers on street corners, but I knew nothing about the man behind the camera.

It was fascinating to research this man. I read many books and online articles about him and about child workers in the early 1900s. I viewed hundreds of Hine's photographs and I found myself wondering what had happened to those sad-faced, barefoot children he captured on film. Did they survive their dangerous jobs? Did they live to become adults?

It was inspiring to learn that the pictures Lewis Hine took for the National Child Labor Committee truly did change the lives of children in the United States – maybe not for the children in his photos, but for children in the future.